THE NATURE KIDS GUIDE TO
GORILLAS

DAVID ANDERSON

LP Media Inc. Publishing

For information address LP Media Inc. Publishing,
30012 Variolite St NW, Princeton MN 55371
www.lpmedia.org

Publication Data

Gorillas
The Nature Kid's Guide to Gorillas — First edition.

Summary: "Learn all about Gorillas, the Nature Kid Way"
— Provided by publisher.

ISBN: 979-8-89818-115-4

[1. Gorillas – Non-Fiction] I. Title.

Title: The Nature Kid's Guide to Gorillas

CONTENTS

MISTY MOUNTAINS

Grunt! A gorilla sits in the cool mountain fog. Mist swirls around her.

Gorillas make their homes in thick forests. There are two types of gorillas, and they live in different places.

Mountain gorillas live high in the mountains. Cool mist covers the trees. The air feels thin and wet. Ferns and vines cover the ground.

Lowland gorillas live in warm, low forests. These places have many swamps. The air feels heavy and damp.

Both types need trees and plants to survive. The forests give them food and shelter. These green places have everything gorillas need.

AFRICAN APES

Thump! A gorilla beats the ground. This powerful ape lives in Africa.

Gorillas only live in Africa.

Along with Lowland and Moutain types, Gorillas have two major varieties: eastern gorillas and western gorillas. Each type lives far apart.

Western gorillas live near the Atlantic Ocean in countries like Cameroon, Gabon, and Congo.

Eastern gorillas live about 560 miles away in Uganda, Rwanda, and the Democratic Republic of Congo.

A gorilla family can have up to 30 members, but most groups have about 10 gorillas.

GENTLE GIANTS

Whoosh! A huge gorilla pushes through the trees. It beats its chest.

Gorillas are the largest apes on Earth. Males are much bigger than females and can weigh up to 500 pounds.

Male gorillas can stand about 5.5 feet high. Females are smaller and weigh around 200 pounds.

Older males have silver hair on their backs. People call them **silverbacks**. Their big bodies help them lead their groups.

A gorilla's arm span can reach over 8 feet. That is wider than most cars!

BUILT BIG

DID YOU KNOW?
A silverback gorilla can be ten times stronger than the strongest human adult.

10

Crack! A gorilla snaps a thick branch with its powerful arms.

Gorillas have powerful bodies. Their arms are longer than their legs. This helps them move through the forest.

Gorilla hands are wide and strong. They can grip branches tightly. Their fingers are thick and padded.

Gorillas have large heads. Their skulls have a bony ridge on top. Strong jaw muscles attach to this ridge. These muscles help gorillas chew tough plants.

Gorillas also have wide, barrel-shaped chests. This shape gives their lungs lots of room.

SHARP
SENSES

Snap! A gorilla turns its head quickly. It hears a sound.

Gorillas have sharp senses. They use sight, sound, and smell to learn about their world.

Gorilla eyes face forward. This helps them see depth. It also helps them spot ripe fruit in the trees.

Gorillas hear very well. Their ears catch soft sounds. They also use smell to find food and sense danger.

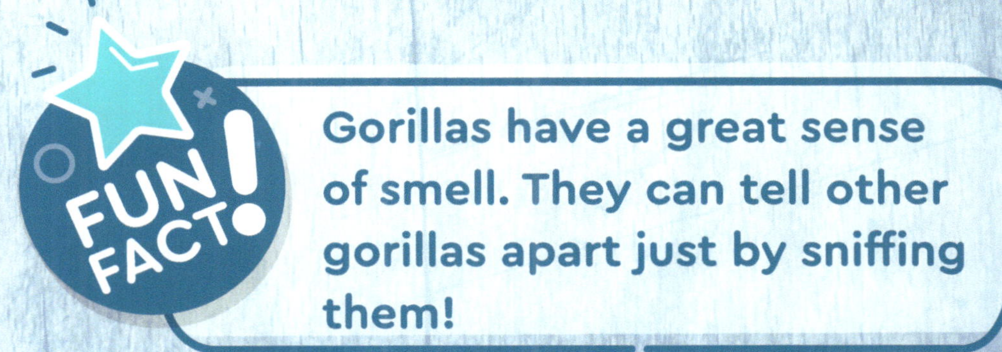

Gorillas have a great sense of smell. They can tell other gorillas apart just by sniffing them!

CHEST
BEATS

Thump, thump, thump! A silverback pounds his chest with cupped hands.

Gorillas beat their chests to **communicate**. The sound can travel far through the forest. Other gorillas can hear it from over half a mile away.

Males beat their chests more often than females. They use cupped hands, not fists, which makes a loud, hollow sound.

Chest beats send many messages. They can warn other males to stay away or show strength.

Gorillas usually beat their chests about 16 times in a row in just a few seconds.

GREEN GRUB

Chomp! A gorilla bites into a leafy stem. It is time for breakfast.

Gorillas eat mostly plants. They spend many hours each day munching on leaves, stems, and shoots.

Gorillas also eat fruit when they can find it. They like wild celery, bamboo, and nettles. Some even eat bark and roots.

Gorillas rarely drink water. They get most of the water they need from juicy plants. Their big bellies help them digest tough leaves.

A gorilla can eat up to 75 pounds of food daily. Talk about eating your greens!

GORILLA GRUNTS
FUN FACT!
Gorillas can make over 20 different sounds to share messages with each other.

Hoot! A gorilla calls out. Others answer back.

Gorillas make many sounds. They grunt, bark, and hoot. Each sound has a meaning. A soft grunt means everything is okay.

Gorillas also use their bodies to talk. When they beat their chests with cupped hands it makes a loud drumming noise. It can be heard far away.

Faces show feelings too. Gorillas open their mouths wide to play. They stare hard when upset. Young gorillas learn these signals by watching adults.

Gorillas even hum when they eat food they like. Happy sounds fill the forest at mealtime.

WATCH OUT!
DID YOU KNOW?
Leopards usually hunt at night when gorillas are sleeping in nests.

Screech! A bird flies away fast. It spotted a leopard nearby.

Gorillas are big and strong. But they have **predators**. Leopards hunt young gorillas. These big cats are fast. They are sneaky too.

Crocodiles can be dangerous near rivers and swamps. Golden eagles have been known to attack baby gorillas.

Adult gorillas are very large. Most predators leave them alone.

But gorillas face another danger. Humans are the biggest threat. Now many gorillas live in protected parks. This helps keep them safe.

STAY SAFE

Growl! A silverback stands tall. He guards his troop.

Gorillas have ways to stay safe. They live in groups led by a silverback. He protects the troop from danger.

When scared, gorillas may run or stay to fight. They move fast through thick plants to escape. Babies ride on their mothers' backs.

Silverbacks use loud roars to scare threats away. They stand up tall on two legs to look even bigger.

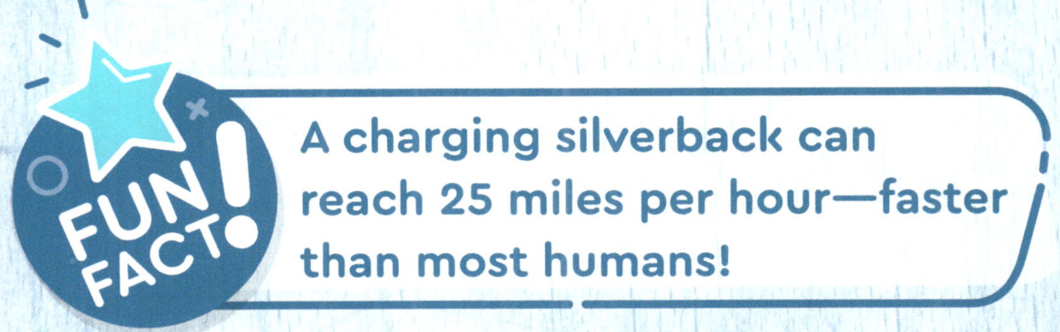

KNUCKLE WALK

Stomp! A gorilla walks on its feet and knuckles through the forest.

Gorillas walk in a special way. They curl their fingers and walk on their knuckles. This is called **knuckle walking**.

Gorillas put their weight on their middle finger bones. This keeps their wrists straight and strong.

Knuckle walking helps gorillas move quickly on the ground while keeping their hands ready to grab food and climb trees.

Gorillas can stand upright but only walk on two legs for short distances. They prefer knuckles!

DAILY LIFE

Stretch! A gorilla yawns wide as the morning sun warms the forest.

Gorillas wake up when the sun rises. Then they start the day by eating breakfast. These apes stay busy all morning!

After eating, gorillas rest during midday. They groom each other and take naps. Young gorillas play while adults relax.

In the afternoon, gorillas eat again. They travel to find fresh plants. At dusk, they build **sleeping nests**.

Gorillas spend about six hours eating each day. They build a new nest every single night!

TROOP TALK

Hoot! A gorilla calls out. Others in the group answer back.

Gorillas live in family groups called troops. A troop usually has one adult male, several females, and their young.

The adult male is called a silverback. He gets this name from the gray hair on his back. He leads the troop.

Troop members stay close together. They look for food and keep babies safe.

Gorillas have best friends! They sit close together and groom each other's fur. Friends stick together for many years.

29

FAMILY TIME

Snort! A silverback gorilla sits near a female and her baby.

Gorillas can have babies at any time of the year. There is no set season for this.

Female gorillas may move to different troops during their lives. They leave their birth group when they grow up.

A silverback may lead a troop for many years. Young males often leave to live alone. They stay alone until they can start their own troop.

Female gorillas usually have their first baby when they are about ten years old.

TINY TOTS
DID YOU KNOW?
A baby gorilla drinks its mother's milk for about three years before eating only plants and leaves.

Squeak! A tiny baby gorilla clings to its mother's chest.

Baby gorillas are tiny at birth. They weigh about four pounds. That is less than most human babies!

Newborns cannot walk. They cannot crawl. They hold onto their mother's fur. Mothers carry babies this way for months. At night, babies sleep in the same nest as their mothers to stay warm and safe.

Baby gorillas grow fast. By four months, they ride on mom's back. They start to crawl. They explore nearby.

Older brothers and sisters help watch the little ones.

GROWING UP

DID YOU KNOW?
Young males who leave home are called blackbacks.

Pull! A young gorilla climbs a vine nearby. Its mother watches closely.

Young gorillas stay with their mothers for several years. They learn by watching and copying adults in the troop.

At around three years old, young gorillas play more with others their age. They wrestle, chase, and climb together. This play helps them grow strong.

Females often stay near their mothers longer. Young males, however, become more independent as they get older. Many male gorillas leave their family group when they are between eight and twelve years old.

FORESTS FALLING

Crack! A tree falls in the forest. A gorilla watches its home disappear.

Gorillas need forests to live. But people cut down trees. They want to make farms. They want wood. This hurts gorilla homes.

When forests get smaller, gorillas have less space. They cannot find enough food. Troops may have to move away.

Moving close to people is risky. Some gorillas get sick from human germs.

Gorillas have lost more than 80 percent of their forest homes. They now survive in just a few protected areas.

37

HELPING
HANDS

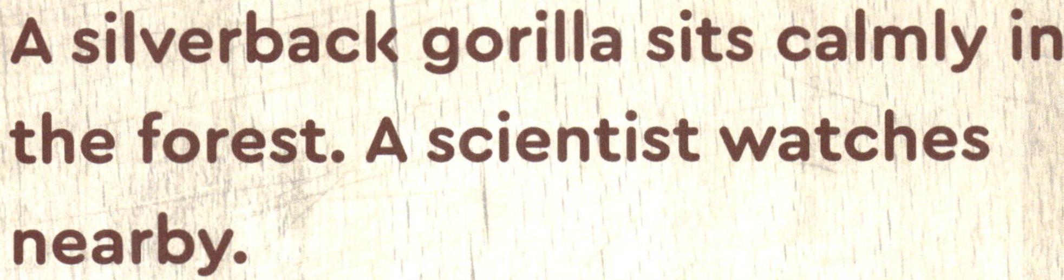

A silverback gorilla sits calmly in the forest. A scientist watches nearby.

People work hard to help gorillas. Rangers guard the forests. They stop hunters.

Scientists help too. They study gorilla families. They learn what gorillas need.

This work is helping. Some gorilla groups are growing. Mountain gorilla numbers have doubled in the last 30 years.

Over one thousand rangers work to protect gorillas in African parks every day.

GLOSSARY

communicate
To share messages or feelings with others

sleeping nests
Beds made of leaves and branches that gorillas build to sleep in each night

predators
Animals that hunt and eat other animals.

knuckle walking
A special way gorillas walk by putting their weight on their curled fingers.

silverback
An older male gorilla with gray hair on his back who leads his family group.